CRUMB AND THE MAGIC OF THE GOLDEN SNOWFLAKE

IT WAS A COLD CHRISTMAS EVE IN THE VILLAGE OF SNOWFALL, AND THE LITTLE DACHSHUND, CRUMB, WAS RUNNING AROUND THE YARD, CHASING HIS OWN FROSTY BREATH. CRUMB WAS FULL OF ENERGY AND CURIOSITY

THE LIGHTS ON THE HOUSES SPARKLED LIKE FALLEN STARS, AND THE AIR SMELLED OF FRESHLY BAKED GINGERBREAD COOKIES. BUT CRUMB HAD A SPECIAL MISSION THAT NIGHT

EVERY CHRISTMAS, THE ANIMALS OF THE VILLAGE PARTICIPATED IN A RACE TO FIND THE GOLDEN SNOWFLAKE, A MAGICAL STAR THAT BROUGHT LUCK FOR THE YEAR TO COME. CRUMB DREAMED OF BEING THE FIRST TO FIND IT

WHILE SNIFFING THE SNOW AND FOLLOWING SQUIRREL TRACKS, HE MET SILVERFEATHER, AN OLD OWL WITH SHIMMERING FEATHERS. "BE CAREFUL, LITTLE FRIEND," WARNED SILVERFEATHER. "CHRISTMAS NIGHT IS FULL OF MYSTERIES."

Be careful, little friiend.

Be careful, little friend.

CRUMB NODDED AND THANKED SILVERFEATHER, BUT HIS ENTHUSIASM DIDN'T WAVER. HE WANTED TO PROVE THAT, EVEN THOUGH HE WAS A DACHSHUND WITH SHORT LEGS, HE HAD A BIG, BRAVE HEART

Be careli, little friend, little friend.

Be careli, little friend,
little friend.

WALKING AMONG SNOW-COVERED FIR TREES, CRUMB HEARD A SOFT JINGLING. "COULD IT BE SANTA'S SLEIGH?" HE WONDERED EXCITEDLY, RUNNING TOWARD THE SOUND

Could it be Santa's sleigh?

Could it be
Santa''s sleigh?

BUT THE JINGLING CAME FROM A LITTLE BELL TIED AROUND THE NECK OF A RED FOX NAMED RUBY. "ARE YOU LOOKING FOR SOMETHING?" RUBY ASKED WITH A MISCHIEVOUS SMILE

Are you looking for something?

Are you looking for something?

"YES, THE GOLDEN SNOWFLAKE!" CRUMB REPLIED, FULL OF HOPE. RUBY SPUN AROUND IN THE SNOW. "THEN YOU'LL NEED A TOUCH OF MAGIC!" SHE SAID, BLOWING A SMALL PUFF OF ENCHANTED SNOW HIS WAY

, Yes, the you touch of magic!

Yes, the Golden Snowflake f mag

CRUMB FELT LIGHT AND HAPPY, AS IF HE HAD WINGS. "GOOD LUCK, LITTLE DACHSHUND," RUBY SAID, DISAPPEARING AMONG THE TREES. THE NIGHT FELT EVEN MORE MAGICAL

Ies, the Golden CHorn Samellette!
Then your'lhen a touch of magic!

Yes, the Golden Golden Snowfllake!
Then you'lhēn a touch of magic!

AS HE WENT ON, CRUMB MET A FAMILY OF WHITE BUNNIES BUILDING SNOWMEN. "HAVE YOU SEEN THE GOLDEN SNOWFLAKE?" HE ASKED, HIS EYES SPARKLING WITH HOPE

"NOT YET," REPLIED THE BIGGEST BUNNY. "BUT IF YOU SEARCH WITH AN OPEN HEART, THE MAGIC OF CHRISTMAS WILL GUIDE YOU." CRUMB THANKED THEM AND CONTINUED HIS JOURNEY

THE FOREST GREW THICKER, AND CRUMB STOPPED TO REST. HE THOUGHT OF HIS FRIENDS AND THE WARM BED WAITING FOR HIM AT HOME. "I MUST FIND IT!" HE ENCOURAGED HIMSELF

Coull it be Santa's sleigh?

Coull it be Santa's sleigh?

SUDDENLY, A SMALL GOLDEN LIGHT APPEARED AT THE TOP OF A TALL FIR TREE. CRUMB HELD HIS BREATH: IT WAS THE GOLDEN SNOWFLAKE! BUT HOW COULD HE REACH IT WITH HIS SHORT LEGS?

WITHOUT LOSING HEART,
CRUMB BEGAN DIGGING IN
THE SNOW AND FOUND AN
OLD FORGOTTEN SLED.
"MAYBE I CAN USE THIS TO
CLIMB!" HE EXCLAIMED,
PULLING IT WITH ALL HIS
STRENGTH

WITH A BIT OF INGENUITY, HE TIED THE SLED WITH VINES AND STARTED BUILDING A RAMP. HE WORKED DETERMINEDLY, EVEN THOUGH THE WIND MADE HIS EARS FREEZE

FINALLY, AFTER MUCH EFFORT, THE RAMP WAS READY. CRUMB TOOK A RUNNING START AND LAUNCHED HIMSELF TOWARD THE TREE, FLYING FOR A MOMENT INTO THE STARRY SKY, LIKE A LITTLE HERO

HE ALMOST REACHED THE TOP, BUT AT THE LAST SECOND, THE SLED STOPPED. CRUMB STRETCHED HIS SNOUT AS FAR AS HE COULD AND... GRABBED THE GOLDEN SNOWFLAKE WITH A TRIUMPHANT BARK!

THE STAR GLOWED IN THE SNOW, LIGHTING UP THE FOREST WITH A WARM GOLDEN LIGHT. THE VILLAGE ANIMALS ARRIVED, AMAZED BY THE LITTLE DACHSHUND'S BRAVERY

"YOU WERE INCREDIBLE, CRUMB!" SAID SILVERFEATHER, NODDING IN RESPECT. EVEN RUBY THE FOX GAVE A PLAYFUL JINGLE OF HER BELL, AMUSED AND PROUD

CRUMB BROUGHT THE GOLDEN SNOWFLAKE TO THE VILLAGE CENTER, AND ALL THE ANIMALS CELEBRATED TOGETHER. THAT NIGHT, UNDER THE STARS, CHRISTMAS IN SNOWFALL WAS THE MOST MAGICAL EVER. AND THE DACHSHUND WITH THE BIG HEART WAS EVERYONE'S HERO

Made in the USA
Coppell, TX
03 December 2024

41707871R00026